Teen Health

Jeannie Kim

SCHOLASTIC INC.

New York   Toronto   London   Auckland   Sydney
Mexico City   New Delhi   Hong Kong   Buenos Aires

Illustrations
Tom Nick Cocotos

Developed by ONO Books in cooperation with Scholastic Inc.

ISBN 0-439-59806-0

7   8   9   10   40   12

Contents

Welcome to This Book

"Fatty food is bad." "Some fats are good." "Get enough sleep." "Don't get too much." "Try to stay positive." "Don't ignore your feelings."

Everyone has advice about how to be healthy. The trouble is they don't always agree. Everyone knows that eating too much junk food is bad. But what if you have it only once in a while? How much sleep do teens really need? Is it normal to have moods that make you feel sad and blue?

This book will give you the facts without the hype. Use what you learn to treat yourself right.

Target Words
These words will help you figure out the best way to stay healthy.

- **nutrients:** substances that the body needs to stay healthy
  Healthy foods provide the nutrients we need.
- **stress:** worry, strain, or pressure
  Having a big test can cause you stress.
- **variety:** a selection of different things
  A healthy diet includes a variety of foods.

Reader Tips
Here's how to get the most out of this book.

- **Charts** Charts are a useful way to organize information. In this book, charts are used to show how to eat in a more healthy way. Look at the chart on page 13. What's one way to get more fruit into your diet?
- **Problem/Solution** This book presents a series of problems about teen health. It then offers solutions about how to solve them. As you read, look for problems and solutions and learn how you can become a more healthy teen.

1

What's Your Health I.Q.?

Take this quiz to find out!

1. How often do you eat fast food?
a. No more than twice a week.
b. Three or four times a week.
c. Five times a week or more.

2. What's your usual exercise routine?
a. I try to work up a sweat every day.
b. Walking from the couch to the refrigerator.
c. I play basketball with my friends once or twice a week.

3. How much sleep do you get every night?
a. Six hours or less.
b. Between six and eight hours.
c. More than eight hours.

4. Do you ever smoke?
a. No, never.
b. I've tried it, but I don't smoke regularly.
c. I smoke two or three times a week or more.

5. How often do you feel really sad?
a. Lately it seems like I feel sad 24/7, sometimes for no reason at all.
b. I feel sad every now and then. But I usually find ways to shake the blues.
c. I'm pretty happy most of the time.

Score!

Check out the answer key on the next page. Then total your score. After that, come back here to see what your score means.

12–15 points: Good work. Read on to see if there's anything you don't already know!

9–11 points: Not bad. See what you can learn.

5–8 points: Watch out! You better shape up before your health starts to suffer.

The answers below are listed in order from healthiest to not so healthy.

Give yourself 3 points if you picked the healthiest answer. Give yourself 2 points if you chose the next healthiest answer. Give yourself 1 point for the least healthy answer.

1. a-b-c. A little fast food won't kill you. Eat a lot of it, though, and you're probably getting too much fat. Find out more in Chapter 2.

2. a-c-b. A little exercise is better than nothing. But an everyday sweat is best. Find out why you need to get moving in Chapter 4.

3. c-b-a. Surprised? Growing bodies—and minds—need up to nine hours of sleep a night. Turn to page 26 for more information.

4. a-b-c. We all know smoking is hard on the lungs. Find out what else suffers in Chapter 5.

5. c-b-a. It's normal to feel sad sometimes. But if you answered "a," you could be depressed. Read Chapter 6 for clues on telling the difference.

(Don't forget to return to the bottom of page 7 to see what your score means.)

The Joys of Junk Food

You don't have to give up the grease to eat right.

Michelle, a fifteen-year-old from Montana, has one big weakness. And she doesn't mind admitting it. She loves junk food, especially potato chips, cookies, and ice cream. Her favorite treat is a milkshake and fries. "I never deny myself my favorite foods," she says.

Even so, Michelle knows how to eat in a healthy way. Sure she chomps on chips. But she also snacks on carrots and apples. She might have a cheeseburger for dinner. But the next night she'll have a salad and a bowl of rice and beans.

The truth is, you can have any food you want and still eat well. The secret is **variety.**

Mix It Up

Food is the fuel for our bodies. It carries **nutrients.** Nutrients are the substances we need to stay strong and healthy. There are five kinds of nutrients: proteins, carbohydrates, vitamins, minerals, and—that's right—fat.

These nutrients play many important roles in your body. Protein helps build muscle. Carbohydrates give you energy. Fat helps your body absorb other nutrients. There are many vitamins and minerals, and they all do different things. For example, vitamin C boosts your **immune system** to help fight off germs. Vitamin B12 helps make blood cells. And the mineral calcium builds strong bones and teeth.

What your body needs is to get the right kind of nutrients in the right amounts. It's not hard to do, and it's not painful. Just make sure to eat a variety of foods. You get protein from cheese, eggs, milk, meat, and beans. Carbohydrates come from foods like bread, cereal, and potatoes. Vitamins and minerals are found in many foods. Fruits and vegetables are the best source. And then, of course, there's fat.

Fat has gotten a bad rap because too much "bad" fat is unhealthy and can lead to disease. But "good" fat can be a great source of energy. It also keeps skin and hair healthy.

So what's bad and what's good when it comes to fat? First you have to know about cholesterol. All fats have some effect on cholesterol levels in your blood. Cholesterol is produced in the liver, and it helps the body produce vitamin D.

There are two kinds of cholesterol. LDL is the bad kind. It sticks to your **artery** walls, making it harder for blood to flow, which can lead to heart disease and other problems. HDL is the good kind. It helps flush LDL out of your body.

So bad fats are the ones that increase the level of LDL in your blood. They're called saturated fats and trans-fatty acids. Fast food usually has these kinds of fats.

But don't swear off fat altogether. Just look for unsaturated fats. They decrease LDL and increase HDL. You can find them in fish, nuts, avocados, and vegetable oils. (See the chart on page 14.)

The bottom line? Enjoy your junk food. But make it a small part of your overall diet.

Use this chart to see what you might eat during a typical day.

What Should I Eat?

Food	How much?	Try this
Fruits	3–4 servings or more (1 serving = 1 piece of fruit, 3/4 cup fruit juice)	• Sweeten your cereal with raisins or berries instead of sugar. • Go for frozen "real fruit" bars.
Vegetables	4–5 servings or more (1 serving = 1 cup leafy greens, 1/2 cup veggies)	• Add lettuce and tomato to sandwiches. • Stash a bag of baby carrots in your backpack.
Grains	6–10 servings (1 serving = 1 slice of bread, 1/2 cup pasta or rice, 1 ounce breakfast cereal)	• Go for whole grain bread or pasta. It has more nutrients and you won't feel hungry as fast.
Dairy or dairy substitute (such as soy milk)	3 servings (1 serving = 1 cup milk or yogurt, 1 1/2 ounces cheese)	• Snack on string cheese. • Have a mini-yogurt and a banana for a quick snack.
Meat, poultry, fish, legumes (beans and peas), nuts, eggs	2–3 servings (1 serving = 1/2 cup legumes, 3 ounces meat or fish, 1 egg, 2 tablespoons nuts)	• Try tuna instead of roast beef for lunch. Fish contains a healthier kind of fat. • Dip apple slices or carrots into peanut butter.

Fat: The Good Guys and the Bad Guys

Type of fat	Main sources	Effects
Saturated	Meat, dairy products, palm and coconut oils	Negative. Raises the level of LDL cholesterol (the "bad" cholesterol) in your blood.
Trans-fatty acids	Margarine, vegetable shortening, packaged baked goods, commercial fried foods like french fries	Negative. Raises LDL cholesterol and lowers HDL cholesterol. Increases heart disease risk and may be even worse than saturated fat.
Polyunsaturated	Corn oil, soybean oil	Mixed. Lowers LDL cholesterol, but also lowers HDL cholesterol.
Monounsaturated	Olive, peanut, and canola oils, avocados, nuts	Positive. Lowers LDL cholesterol and raises HDL cholesterol (the "good" cholesterol).
Omega-3 fatty acids (a type of unsaturated fat)	Fish, flaxseed, walnuts	Positive. Protects against heart disease and helps keep the heartbeat steady. Essential to building a healthy body, including the eyes and brain.

The Truth About Diets

"Lose 15 pounds in five days!" "Try the AMAZING new fat-burning diet!" "Get slim with the super-duper all-grapefruit diet!" Ever been tempted by one of those crazy schemes? Beware! Here's what you really need to know about dieting:

- The average teen needs 2,000 to 2,500 calories a day. But some diets limit you to 1,000 calories a day. That's not healthy. Calories are the fuel your body needs to grow and create energy. If you don't get enough calories, you'll feel tired, cranky, or weak.

- Dieting can leave you short on important nutrients, like calcium and iron. (Iron helps red blood cells carry oxygen throughout your body.)

- Fad diets generally don't work. One study found that teen girls who dieted were more likely to gain weight.

If you're thinking of going on a diet, check with your doctor. If she says you're overweight, ask her to suggest an exercise program and a sensible diet.

3

Vegging Out

A growing number of teens are skipping meat. Here's why.

Imagine life without juicy hamburgers or fried chicken. Sound tough? Not to Heidi, a sixteen-year-old from Colorado. Three years ago, she stopped eating meat. "I've always loved animals," she says. "I thought it was cruel to kill another living thing just so I could have a meal."

Alex, who's seventeen and lives in New York, has also gone meatless. But he decided to take it further. "I realized that if I cared about animal rights, I shouldn't eat anything that comes from animals," he says. So Alex doesn't drink milk. He doesn't eat eggs, cheese, or honey.

Heidi and Alex are vegetarians. In other words, they completely skip meat. And by not eating *any* animal products, such as milk, butter, and cheese,

Alex is a vegan. There are about 19 million vegetarians in the United States, and a growing number of them are teens.

There are many reasons why people go veggie. Like Alex and Heidi, some hate the thought of killing animals. Others say animals that are raised to produce food are treated badly.

Many also believe vegetarianism is better for the environment. Raising animals for food requires a lot of land. Vegetarians say we could produce more food if we planted crops on that land. "I became a vegetarian because I thought killing animals was wrong," says Alex. "But when I found out about the environmental benefits, I was even more convinced."

The Right Way to Veg Out

Going veggie can be a healthy choice. There are two big advantages for your body:

- **Less fat:** Red meat is heavy in saturated fat. So most vegetarians get less of this fat. As a result, they tend to have less heart disease, and they're less likely to be overweight.

© Tim Bath/Kokomo Tribune/AP/Wide World Photos

Animals who are raised for food are often kept in pens like these. Some people think this is cruel.

- **More vegetables:** Vegetarians tend to eat more veggies, of course. And veggies are packed with nutrients that fight disease. Studies show that they can even reduce the risk of **cancer.**

Still, it's easy for a no-meat diet to fall short on important nutrients. Here are two that are often skipped:

- **Protein:** This nutrient provides energy that feeds and helps form muscles. But vegetarians don't eat the foods that are the typical sources of protein—meat, fish, and eggs. So they need good substitutes like dairy products. Beans, nuts, and soy products provide protein as well. They are a must for vegans, who don't eat dairy.
- **Calcium:** This is a mineral that builds strong bones and teeth. It's available in milk and cheese. But vegans need to find other sources. These might include spinach, black beans, tofu, and **fortified** orange juice.

No-Meat Musts

Here's a chart with some other meaty nutrients—and where to get them from animal and non-animal sources.

Nutrient	Animal source	Non-animal source
protein	beef, poultry, fish, eggs, or dairy products	beans, tofu, tempeh, nuts, wheat gluten, or legumes and whole grains eaten together
calcium	dairy products	green leafy vegetables, black beans, tofu, or fortified orange juice
iron	beef or chicken	kale, tofu, black beans, soybeans, or broccoli
zinc	beef or yogurt	wheat germ or beans
vitamin B12	oily fish (like salmon) or dairy products	vitamins, fortified soy milk, or brewer's yeast

Heads Up!

Plan a meal that would give a vegetarian all of these nutrients. Can you do the same for a vegan?

Work It Out

What's the secret to being stronger, happier, and more energetic? Exercise.

According to more than one survey, most teens are couch potatoes. One study says that only two out of ten teens work out for more than twenty minutes a day.

The other eight don't know what they're missing. Just ask Chris, a seventeen-year-old from Illinois. He used to spend most of his free time in front of the TV. Then one day, he decided to try running. "The first time, I could only run for around thirty seconds," he says. "I got tired right away." But Chris kept at it.

Now Chris runs for thirty minutes almost every day. He says he has more energy. He's stronger. He looks better. And he's found a great way to blow off steam.

Here are other ways exercise is good for you:

- **It makes hearts healthy.** Your heart is a pump. Its job is to get blood to all parts of the body. The blood carries fuel for your muscles in the form of oxygen. The stronger your heart is, the more fuel it pumps. The more fuel you get, the more energy you have. The best exercise for your heart is aerobic exercise. That's any activity that speeds up your heart and your breathing—like running or swimming.

- **It makes you stronger.** Muscles get stronger if you use them. Running, biking, or doing push-ups and pull-ups will do it. You can also strengthen muscles by lifting weights. But lifting can put a strain on growing bodies. If you want to try weights, get help from a coach, trainer, or gym teacher.

Heads Up!

Think of two examples of aerobic exercise that you do, like climbing stairs. Then think of two activities you do that aren't aerobic.

The trick to getting enough exercise is choosing an activity that you really enjoy.

- **It makes you more flexible.** Some kinds of exercise, such as yoga or gymnastics, stretch your muscles. This makes your body more flexible, which helps you avoid injuries.
- **It's the key to healthy weight.** When you exercise, you burn off calories. You also make muscle. Muscle burns more calories than fat. If you have more muscle, you'll burn more calories even when you're not exercising.
- **It boosts your mood.** When you exercise, your body makes endorphins. These chemicals cut down on pain signals sent between your nerve cells. That, in turn, reduces pain and makes you feel better.
- **It protects you from disease.** Working out helps prevent heart disease, **diabetes,** and other diseases.

Get Moving!

Want a stronger body? Work toward getting twenty to thirty minutes of exercise every day. You can break it up into shorter workouts if you want. Walking or biking home from school could count as five to ten minutes. You might add another six to ten minutes doing jumping jacks and push-ups during TV commercials. You can sneak in exercise in other ways, too. Take the stairs instead of the elevator or escalator. Offer to carry in the groceries. Park at the opposite end of the mall from your favorite store.

Here's the best way to work out. Warm up slowly for a few minutes, then work out at three-quarters of your maximum effort. You don't want to push yourself or you could hurt your muscles and your joints. When you're done, do some stretches. This will help your muscles stay flexible. Make sure you stretch after you exercise. If you stretch before you exercise, your muscles won't be loose and you could tear them.

Exercise sensibly and your body will get stronger. You'll be able to workout harder and longer if you keep at it. So, go ahead. Get moving!

—Heads Up!——

Are you getting enough exercise? If not, how many ways can you think of to get exercise into your day?

Snooze or Lose

Do you get enough sleep? Probably not. The average teen sleeps six or seven hours a night. But most teens actually need nine hours or more.

Research shows that skipping sleep is a bad idea. It can even be dangerous. Lack of sleep makes it harder to concentrate in class. It makes it harder for the body to fight off disease. And it can lead to car accidents and other accidents.

To get a good night's sleep, try these tips:

- **Create a cozy space.** Before getting into bed, make your room as dark and quiet as possible.

- **Chill out.** Do something calming, such as reading or listening to quiet music. Don't watch TV or talk on the phone right before bed.

- **Cut down on caffeine.** Lay off the coffee or cola, especially after six in the evening.

- **Exercise regularly.** But don't work out right before bed.

- **Stick to a schedule.** You're never too old to have a bedtime. Go to bed and get up at the same times every day, even on weekends.

5

Smoke Screen

The facts are in and they still say smoking is really, really bad for you.

Everyone has seen the ads and read the warnings about smoking. Still, people choose to light up. And a lot of brand new smokers are teens. Nearly three out of every ten high school students smoke.

Take Rachel*, sixteen, from Colorado, who started smoking last year. "Some of my older friends smoke, and they bought cigarettes for me," she says. Now she smokes every day, before and after school. When her parents aren't home, she smokes nonstop.

Rachel says she knows the risks. "Every time I light up, I think that I should quit. I want to quit so badly, but I just can't stop."

*not her real name

The Truth About Smoking

The bad effects of smoking are well known. But if you need some more reasons to keep from starting or to kick the habit, here are the facts. And they are not pretty.

- **Smoking makes you ugly.** Cigarettes have tar in them. That's the black stuff they use to make roads. It can stain your teeth yellow. Smoking also shrinks blood vessels in your skin. That means your skin doesn't get enough oxygen and other nutrients. The result? Premature lines and wrinkles. And don't forget the bad breath.

- **Smoking wrecks your lungs.** Cigarette smoke contains 4,000 chemicals. Some of them stop your lungs from growing properly. So you'll never get as much oxygen to your body as a nonsmoker. Smokers also get more colds and coughs. Their lungs don't fight off infection as well. And then there's lung cancer. It kills 170,000 people a year. And smokers are 20 times more likely to get it than nonsmokers.

American Lung Association

Scholastic Photo Archive

See the two lungs above. The one on the left belongs to a smoker. The one on the right is healthy. Need we say more?

- **Smoking damages your heart.** Smokers have more heart disease. Smoking shrinks blood vessels. That means your heart has to work harder. It has to pump 10 to 25 more times per minute. Over the years, that can really add up. And all that extra work wears your heart muscle out.
- **Smoking makes you weak.** Teens who smoke have less endurance. They get worn out faster because they can't get as much oxygen into their lungs. "When I play softball, I get dizzy and I have to take breaks more often," says Rachel.

Excuses, Excuses

So why do people still light up? Here's what they say.

Excuse #1: "I only smoke once in a while." Cigarettes contain a drug called nicotine. It makes a smoker feel alert and relaxed. But nicotine is a very **addictive** drug. That's why cigarettes are so hard to quit. And that's why it's surprisingly easy to get hooked on them. Smoking once a month can do it, says one study.

Excuse #2: "I'll quit later." Eight out of ten adult smokers started when they were teens. The younger a smoker starts, the more likely he or she is to get addicted. And quitting is easier said than done. Here's a reality check from Rachel. "When I try to stop, I get really bad cravings for cigarettes," she says. "I also have mood swings and I'm hard to be around. That happens if I go two days without a cigarette."

Excuse #3: "It's my body." Some smokers say they know smoking is bad for them, but they don't care. They think they should be able to do anything they want to their own body. But secondhand smoke affects everyone who breathes it. It bothers their eyes and throats. It can cause attacks in asthma sufferers. Some studies say it might cause cancer. In addition, health care for smokers is expensive. And everyone helps pay for their hospital bills with higher insurance rates.

Heads Up!

Name five health problems that are connected with smoking.

Taking on Tobacco

American tobacco companies earn more than $45 billion a year. But that profit has a high cost in human life. About 430,000 Americans die each year from illnesses related to cigarette smoking.

So, some people have decided to fight back. They've started taking tobacco companies to court. They claim that the companies misled the public for a long time about the health effects of cigarettes. And they want cigarette companies to take responsibility for their actions.

The lawyers for the tobacco companies argue that people have known for years that smoking can be unhealthy. They say that smokers know the risks and choose to smoke anyway. It's not the tobacco companies' fault.

But memos written by executives at tobacco companies tell another story. The memos show that tobacco executives knew that cigarettes were addictive long before they admitted it to the public. And that they may have looked for ways of making cigarettes *even more addictive.* That didn't make them look very good in court.

By 2003, big tobacco companies have already paid more than $240 billion in damages.

6

Dealing With Feelings

*Ever feel like your emotions are out of control?
You're not alone.*

Do you get upset over small things? (Well, maybe other people think they are small.) And do you go from being happy one minute to being sad the next? If so, it could mean one important thing.

You're completely normal.

In fact, a teenager's body goes through some pretty big changes. And those changes can affect your mood.

Teenage bodies make lots of chemicals called **hormones.** These chemicals produce physical changes in the body—for example, those hairs on your chin if you're a guy, and those new curves if you're a girl. But these hormones also trigger emotional ups and downs.

When Darkness Falls

The **stress** of daily life gets to everyone from time to time. And it can be especially hard on teens. But for some teens, feelings of sadness get very intense. And they won't go away.

Angela knows the feeling well. A few years ago she started feeling like no one cared about her. "I liked this guy, but he didn't return my feelings," remembers Angela, who's now sixteen and lives in Ohio. "And my family was never around. My older brother and sister were always getting in trouble. I felt so alone."

Angela started to spend most of her time in her bedroom. There, she listened to music and cried. She hardly ate. And she stopped hanging out with friends.

Angela wasn't just suffering through a bad mood. She was depressed.

Depression is a serious illness. Depressed people may feel sad or hopeless for weeks, months, or years. Angela's depression has lasted for nearly four years. "After a friend of mine died, it got so bad that I wanted to die, too."

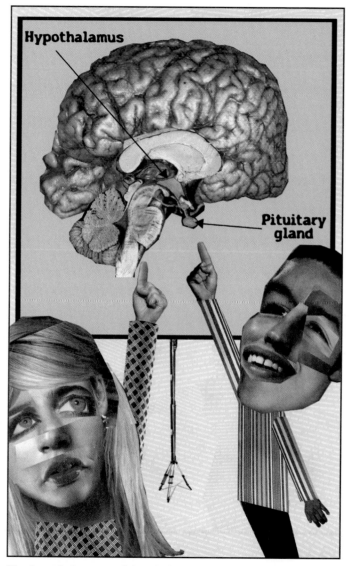

Hypothalamus

Pituitary gland

The hypothalamus and the pituitary gland produce hormones that can affect your mood.

Angela finally told her mom how she was feeling. Her mom took her to a doctor who talked to Angela about her problem and then gave her a kind of medicine called an antidepressant. Antidepressants change the balance of certain chemicals in the brain. Angela also started seeing a **psychiatrist.** There, she could talk about her problems. "Some days are still really hard, but it's getting better," she says.

What Causes Depression?

Depression can have many different causes. Sometimes a sad event, like the death of a close friend, can lead to depression. Other times a person just starts to feel down, even if nothing bad has happened. Or it may be **genetic**—passed on from your parents to you through your genes.

Whatever the cause, depression is a disease that needs treatment. You can't just "snap out of it." And you shouldn't feel embarrassed to ask for help. Besides, you're not alone. About 16 million Americans a year suffer from depression. Seeing a therapist for depression should be no different than going to the doctor for a broken arm.

Some people, like Angela, use medication to help them get through depression. Other people work through it with talk therapy. Find a doctor or school counselor you trust. Together you can help figure out what works best for you.

Depression Signs

How do you tell the difference between a bad mood and depression? Check out the chart below. It will show the difference.

Bad Mood	Depression
Feeling bummed when you make a mistake	Feeling like things will never be right again
Having a good cry when you're upset	Crying for no reason or feeling sad all the time
Needing some alone time once in a while	Pulling away from family or friends
Sleeping late because you're feeling tired or lazy	Sleeping all day because you don't want to get out of bed
Wishing that you could change things in your life	Thinking about physically hurting yourself
Feeling this way for a few minutes, hours, or days	Feeling this way for two weeks or more

Stressed Out?

Even if you're not depressed, you might be feeling more stressed out than usual. Maybe you've been fighting with your parents a lot. Maybe the pressures of school have gotten too intense. This can leave you feeling extra nervous or tense. It may not be serious now, but you don't want to ignore it. If stress builds up, it can lead to depression. The good news is that stress can be treated before it gets you down. Here are five ways to get it under control.

1. **Talk it out.** Talking to someone you trust can help you work through what's bothering you.

2. **Work it out.** Exercise can help you feel better. (Remember those endorphins?)

3. **Sleep it off.** Don't try to do too much. Being tired can make you more irritable.

4. **Take a breather.** When you're angry or frustrated, stop and take a few deep breaths and count to ten.

5. **Have fun.** Don't be so serious. Make time to do stuff you love.

How *Not* to Deal With Stress

Some people use drugs or alcohol to deal with stress. Some want to numb themselves out so that they can't feel anything. Others try to control their feelings artificially. But here's what really happens when you do that.

Alcohol and drugs that relax you are called depressants. They slow down the **nervous system,** including your brain. They can cause depression or make it worse.

Drugs that perk you up are called stimulants. They make your heart race and interfere with your ability to sleep. They end up leaving you feeling tense, jumpy, and even **paranoid.**

The effects on your body are even more serious. You can risk addiction to alcohol or pills. You also risk sudden death from an overdose or a bad reaction. That is true for any drug, including alcohol. And if you take an illegal drug, you have no way to know how strong it is, or what's really in it.

And here's another reality check. Every year, thousands of teens end up in the emergency room—dead—from using alcohol or drugs.

Does this sound less stressful to you?

7

Body Art Smarts

Read this before you let someone stick needles into your skin.

Body art is all the rage. Those tattoos and body piercings might look cool, but are they safe? Here are the real risks and ways to protect yourself.

Tattoos: Getting Under Your Skin

Gemma, at age seventeen, designed her own tattoo. She has a fairy on the small of her back. "I'd love to say I was really hard core and wasn't afraid," she says. "But that would be a huge lie. I kept thinking, 'I must be crazy. Am I really going to let a random stranger use needles to inject ink into me a billion times?'"

Needles? Yep. That's how tattoos work. A tattoo artist uses a tool with several small needles. An electric motor powers the needles. They prick the skin thousands of times a minute. This punches ink into the flesh. "It was kind of like being stung repeatedly by a wasp," says Gemma.

Because the ink is in your skin, tattoos are permanent. "A lot of younger people get tattooed just as a fashion statement, and then end up hating it," Gemma says.

If you do change your mind, you can remove a tattoo. But the process is expensive and painful. A doctor uses a laser beam to zap the **pigment.** Patients usually have 5 to 15 treatments over the course of a year. The laser treatment can leave a scar. And it may not completely remove the tattoo.

Getting a tattoo can be risky, too. Why? Unclean needles can give you serious diseases like **HIV** and **hepatitis B.** Or you may have an **allergic reaction** to the tattoo ink. This can cause itching and rashes. Skin infections may cause redness, oozing, swelling, bleeding, and scarring.

Heads Up!

What are the risks involved with getting a tattoo? What are the benefits?

It's also important to take good care of the tattoo as it heals. Otherwise it may get infected. "I didn't follow the aftercare instructions properly, and as a result, my tattoo scabbed up and got all nasty, and bits of it fell off," says Gemma.

If you still want to get tattooed, here's what you'll need to know. First, find a licensed tattoo artist. Call your local health department. Ask them how you can find one in your area.

If you are under 18, you will probably need your parents' permission. Your parents will have to sign a form. It says that you and your parents understand the risks and are willing to take your chances. That way, if anything goes wrong, the tattoo artist will not be held responsible.

Once you find a licensed tattoo artist, visit the studio. Look around. Is it clean? But don't judge by looks alone. Ask questions about health and safety. A good shop should be happy to explain how they keep their customers safe. And be sure they use an autoclave. That's a device used to **sterilize** equipment. You don't want anyone to use dirty needles on you—ever!

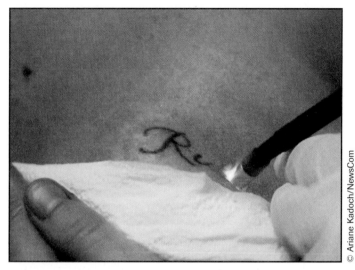

Tattoos can be removed. They are burnt off by a laser.

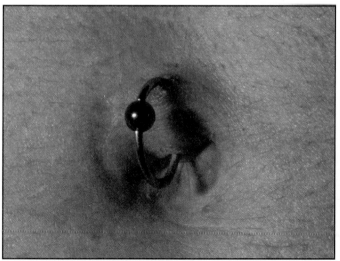

Piercings often get infected. Infections are painful and can leave scars that look like bumps.

Piercing: The Hole Truth

Like tattoos, piercings are popular. Nathaniel, who's fourteen and lives in New York, started with his ears. "My friends dared me to do it," he says. "They bet ten bucks apiece that I wouldn't get both ears pierced."

Nathaniel did it, but he admits he made a mistake. He let a friend do the piercing. And the friend used a regular needle. It wasn't sterilized. "My right ear got all infected and ugly looking," he says.

Now he's thinking about getting a tongue stud when he turns sixteen. But this time he plans to go to a real piercing studio.

Piercing is pretty simple. A body part is punctured with a sharp tool. Then a piece of jewelry is placed in the hole. The piercing can take from a few weeks to several months to heal. A belly button piercing can take over a year to heal. Clothing and movement can **irritate** it. This can be painful and cause it to get infected.

There are health risks to all piercings. Just like with tattoos, unclean needles can spread diseases.

Never let anyone use a "piercing gun" on you. They aren't sterile. Any other tools the piercer uses should be brand new or sterilized in an autoclave.

Even when the tools are clean, new piercings can easily become infected. The area may swell up, turn red, and feel hot and painful. And it can fill up with **pus,** a yellowish fluid.

Some people also get bad scars or allergic reactions from piercings. And tongue piercings have their own special problems. The inside of your mouth is warm, dark, and wet. This makes it more likely that the piercing will get infected. Tongue studs may also chip teeth.

Usually you need a parent's permission to be pierced if you're under eighteen. And don't get pierced (or tattooed) at a place that doesn't follow the law. Who knows what other rules they might be breaking?

Heads Up!

Based on this chapter, what advice would you give a friend who wanted to get her belly button pierced?

Glossary

addictive *(adjective)* causing the need to use a substance regularly (p. 30)

allergic reaction *(noun)* a bad reaction that happens when someone is extra sensitive to a substance (p. 41)

artery *(noun)* a tube that carries blood from the heart to other parts of the body (p. 11)

cancer *(noun)* a disease where some cells in the body grow faster than normal cells and kill healthy organs and tissue (p. 19)

diabetes *(noun)* a disease in which there is too much sugar in the blood (p. 24)

fortified *(adjective)* something added that makes a substance stronger, better (p. 19)

genetic *(adjective)* having been passed down from parent to child by genes (p. 36)

hepatitis B *(noun)* a liver disease that is spread by infected blood (p. 41)

HIV *(noun)* virus that causes AIDS (Acquired Immunodeficiency Syndrome) (p. 41)

hormones *(noun)* chemicals in your body that affect the way you grow and develop (p. 33)

immune system *(noun)* system that protects the body from foreign substances (bacteria, viruses); includes thymus, spleen, lymph nodes, and antibodies (p. 10)

irritate *(verb)* to make sore or sensitive (p. 44)

nervous system *(noun)* the brain, spinal cord, and nerves (p. 39)

nutrient *(noun)* a substance the body needs to stay healthy (p. 10)

paranoid *(adjective)* feeling fearful that people are out to get you when they're not (p. 39)

pigment *(noun)* a substance that gives color to something (p. 41)

pus *(noun)* a thick, yellow liquid that comes out of an infected wound or sore (p. 45)

psychiatrist *(noun)* a doctor who specializes in mental health (p. 36)

sterilize *(verb)* to clean something so thoroughly that you make it free from germs and dirt (p. 42)

stress *(noun)* worry, strain, or pressure (p. 34)

variety *(noun)* a selection of different things (p. 9)

Index